Mrs. Fickle's Pickles

Lori Ries

Illustrated by **Nancy Cote**

BOYDS MILLS PRESS

HONESDALE, PENNSYLVANIA

Special thanks to friends Kent Brown, Larry Rosler, and Eileen Spinelli. Also to my father-in-law, Edward Ries, who enjoys a good deli pickle as much as I do. To my family, thank you for your continued love and support.
—L. R.

To S. M.,
my favorite "silly pickle"!
—N. C.

Text copyright © 2006 by Lori Ries
Illustrations copyright © 2006 by Nancy Cote

Boyds Mills Press, Inc.
A Highlights Company
815 Church Street
Honesdale, Pennsylvania 18431
Printed in China

Library of Congress Cataloging-in-Publication Data

Ries, Lori Anne.
Mrs. Fickle's pickles / Lori Anne Ries ; illustrated by Nancy Cote.— 1st ed.
p. cm.
Summary: Rhyming text with illustrations tells how Mrs. Fickle likes her pickles.
ISBN-13: 978-1-59078-195-1 (hardcover : alk. paper)
[1. Pickles—Fiction. 2. Stories in rhyme.] I. Cote, Nancy, ill. II. Title.

PZ8.3.R443Mr 2006
[E]—dc22

2006000768

First edition, 2006
The text of this book is set in 24-point Sabon.
The illustrations are done in gouache.

Visit our Web site at www.boydsmillspress.com

10 9 8 7 6 5 4 3 2 1

Mrs. Fickle likes her pickles.

She plants each tiny seed.

Mrs. Fickle likes her pickles.

They're growing fast indeed.

Mrs. Fickle likes her pickles.

She plants them with great care.

Mrs. Fickle
likes her pickles.

She'll bring them to the fair.

Mrs. Fickle likes her pickles.

They hold the flavor in.

Mrs. Fickle likes her pickles.

She hopes that they will win.

Mrs. Fickle likes her pickles.

Pickles are lots of fun.

But Mrs. Fickle LOVES her pickles . . .

sitting on her tongue.